Great Danger

A Writer's Guide to Building Suspense

Great Danger

A Writer's Guide to Building Suspense

by

Ken Pelham

Cover Art and Design:
Jennifer Pelham

Cover Imagery Sources:
Petradr
Martin Wessely

Cover Typefaces:
Bebas Neue by Dharma Type
Braeside by Typodermic Fonts Inc.

Acknowledgments

Thanks are in order to the members of the Maitland Writers Group, to all the writers who've attended my writing workshops, and to the libraries and staff who've graciously allowed me the use of their facilities in which to give them. And as always, my undying gratitude to Amy, Jennifer, and Laura, for their love, support, and jambalaya with shrimp and Andouille sausage.

Table of Contents

PART I: Understanding Suspense

...'tis true that we are in great danger; the greater therefore should our courage be.

—William Shakespeare, *Henry V*

Suspense... What the Heck is it?

Everyone has a good idea of what suspense is, but what exactly *is* it? What causes it? Most importantly for writers, how do we harness it?

For starters, *Merriam-Webster Dictionary* gives us a definition.

Suspense (noun): a feeling or state of nervousness or excitement caused by wondering what will happen.

Simple enough. Doesn't yield any real understanding, though.

It's fair to say that suspense is a form of uncertainty. Furthermore, suspense is bound at the hip to fear. Although they are not one and the same, the connection is powerful.

Forget all the hooey from **Jedi knights** about fear. Fear is in you, they say. Leads to anger and hate, blah blah blah. Be free of fear, blah blah blah. The Jedi are idiots.

Fear is *good.* It's a natural response to harmful stimuli. It's not there for no reason. Millions of years in the school of biological hard knocks have left us hard-wired to experience fear. It's evolutionary and built in for survival.

It's nothing to be ashamed of.

When faced with life-threatening danger (and really, all danger is life-threatening), our responses fall into two camps; fight or flight. Both responses release a cocktail of chemicals in the body. The reactions to these chemicals essentially define *fear.*

Again, fear is good. Three and a half million years ago, **Australopithecines**, scratching out an existence under the blazing Central African sun, regularly fought or fled lions, leopards, hyenas, snakes, and crocodiles. Even oversized eagles killed and ate the rather diminutive Australopithecines. Two options, fight or flight. Flight proved the most successful choice, most often. Fighting these toothy horrors generally did not end well.

Fight or flight. These options have been passed down through the millennia.

I knew a couple of guys in high school that claimed they weren't afraid of anything. I didn't believe it then and I don't believe it now. They were liars and knuckleheads. Fear is normal. Having no fear is abnormal, so if abnormality is how they choose to be seen, so be it. There *are* rare, exceptional persons who seemingly have no fear, and we'll get to how they're abnormal.

As with our every emotion, fear originates in the brain. Small structures called the **amygdala** seem to be the home of fear. When a sabertooth cat snarls and gathers itself to pounce upon you, the amygdala goes to work. It raises the alarm and sends out orders. It shuts down resource-consuming nonessential functions and reallocates resources (good management skills, that). It calls on the **hypothalamus**, which in turns calls the **pituitary gland**, which in turn calls the **thyroid** and **adrenal systems**. The thyroid gland raises your metabolism. The **pupils** dilate, enabling you to observe finer detail. The **heart** pumps faster, the blood pressure rises, making fuel more readily available. The **liver** breaks down glycogen for energy; the **spleen** pumps out white blood cells in order to doctor you after the sabertooth bites off your leg; the **bladder** and **colon** prepare for evacuation (you piss and shit your pants or loincloth), perhaps to make you more agile and swift, perhaps to lessen the severity of injury; the **bronchioles** in the lungs dilate, grabbing more oxygen; and perhaps most importantly, the **adrenal medulla** goes into overdrive, squirting adrenaline and its trusty sidekick noradrenaline like there's no tomorrow (because there likely *isn't*), making you a turbocharged version of your normal mild-mannered self.

Perhaps just as importantly as getting you through this initial danger, the amygdala also stores memory of the incident in a data file for future access. Maybe saves a jpeg or two. It shares these files with the **hippocampus**, and between them they preserve the long-term memory so that you're better prepared to deal with the next sabertooth you happen upon.

I mentioned the rare individuals that apparently don't experience fear. One clinical case involved a woman who suffered from a physical deterioration of the amygdala, to the point where it had pretty much disappeared entirely. Tests showed that she really did fear nothing, and would engage in dangerous tasks without thinking twice about it. She had clear memories of being terribly afraid of all the usual things as a child.

In lab experiments, the amygdala have been surgically removed from monkeys. The same monkeys which previously had a deathly, evolved, and extreme fear of snakes, now would handle or swat the snakes without hesitation.

So we know fear is tied to the amygdala. The lack of one indicates a lack of the other. A lack of either should rightfully be considered a handicap, as mammalian individuals —as well as entire species— without fear will come to an abrupt end.

Tempering fear, the remaining component of suspense is hope. This, perhaps, is what makes the fear bearable. Hope, the anticipation of positive outcomes, is why we soldier on.

The Paradox of Suspense

We enjoy suspense in our various forms of entertainment. But why?

Why would anyone enjoy uncertainty and fear? Are those things pleasant?

Maybe. The release of chemicals throughout the body can certainly feel different. The adrenaline rush, the accelerated heartbeat, the heightened senses… those might be enjoyed, particularly when we're aware that they're induced from a fantasy rather than a real and immediate threat.

Another paradox. If suspense involves uncertainty, how can we feel suspense while watching or reading a work of suspense we've already seen or read?

I remember as a teen the drama surrounding the disastrous and nearly tragic Apollo 13 mission. I've watched the **Ron Howard** film of the same name maybe a half-dozen times. I've read the 1994 **Jim Lovell** and **Jeffrey Kluger** book (originally titled *Lost Moon: The Perilous Voyage of Apollo 13*), upon which the 1995 movie is adapted. I know full well how the event plays out. Yet every time I see the movie,

I'm on the edge of my seat, hoping, praying that they'll get out alive.

This is of course a sign of great storytelling. Bad storytelling, and you don't give a rat's ass even the first time you see or read something.

Psychologists haven't figured this thing out yet. There are at least four competing theories as to how and why we can find suspense in something with which we're familiar. I won't rehash them all here, but will point out that one theory states that it's not suspense (and certainly not fear) we enjoy, but anticipation of the relief (and fun chemicals) when it's all over and the danger is past. It's easy to anticipate something you know *will* end well.

Suffice to say, the enjoyment and paradoxes of suspense are mysteries in themselves, but darned good ones for makers of fictions.

Hitchcock on Suspense…

In 1962, youthful French director **Francois Truffaut** enticed legendary **Alfred Hitchcock** to sit for a lengthy set of on-camera interviews about the nature and art of suspense in film. Hitchcock did not consider himself a director of mysteries, and was quite clear that what he worked in was suspense. He felt that he had directed only one movie that could be classified as a traditional mystery. He furthermore explained that the traditional mystery was constructed as an intellectual exercise, whereas suspense took its power from emotion. He made no apologies for this, although some eggheads might argue that we should always strive toward lofty intellectual efforts. The sad fact of our species is that emotion is stronger by far than intellect. Look at history if you need corroboration. What may be bad for our well-being, however, is powerful (and good) in fiction. We are challenged by intellect. We are *moved* by emotion.

Hitchcock goes on to explain what makes a scene suspenseful, and that suspense doesn't require keeping your audience in the dark. Characters perhaps, but not audience. As Hitchcock illustrates it:

> *"There is a distinct difference between 'suspense' and 'surprise.'*
>
> *We are now having a very innocent little chat. Let's suppose that there is a bomb underneath this table between us. Nothing happens, and then all of a sudden, "Boom!" There is an explosion. The public is surprised, but prior to this surprise, it has seen an absolutely ordinary scene, of no special consequence. Now, take a suspense situation. The bomb is underneath the table and the public knows it, because they have seen the anarchist place it there. The public is aware the bomb is going to explode at one o'clock*

> *and there is a clock in the decor. The public can see that it is a quarter to one. In these conditions this same innocuous conversation becomes fascinating because the public is participating in the scene. The audience is longing to warn the characters on the screen: "You shouldn't be talking about such trivial matters. There is a bomb beneath you and it is about to explode!"*
>
> *In the first case we have fifteen seconds of surprise at the moment of the explosion. In the second we have fifteen minutes of suspense. The conclusion is that whenever possible the public must be informed."*

Mystery vs. Suspense vs. Thriller

"Suspense" as an idea differs from "Suspense" as a genre. Suspense is a part of all fiction (or should be) to some extent.

To the detriment of both readers and writers, the industry is determined to slap labels on fiction. Genres abound. Sub-genres abound. Sub-*sub* genres abound. What you write is going to get a label. Don't let that define you or restrict you.

But since the labels are there, let's take a quick look at the conventional labels.

A browse through the bookstore might reveal that **Robert B. Parker** is in the "Mystery" aisle, while **Mary Higgins Clark** might not be; she's labeled "Suspense." Maybe even "Romantic Suspense." **Ken Follett** might dwell in the "Fiction" aisle, as if those other genres aren't fiction.

Then there's "Crime Fiction." Some like to use that as the umbrella term to cover all the others. However, a lot of novels these days are called "crime fiction," feeding the misperception that they're in some special, separate genre. I suspect this is pure marketing, as the bean-counters desperately want to avoid calling something simply "mystery." "Mystery," to them, sounds too pretty, too safe, too old-fashioned apparently, whereas "crime fiction" somehow sounds grittier. Okayyy…

Let's narrow our focus from all fiction to three genre labels, mystery, suspense, and thriller, and see what distinguishes one from the other.

The traditional, classic mystery dates pretty much from **Edgar Allen Poe's** "The Murders in the Rue Morgue" (1841). Poe established the ground rules and conventions with that story, giving us the so-called "locked room" mystery, the puzzling clues and evidence, and the shrewd detective. This found immediate success and inspired the traditional mystery writers to follow. **Arthur Conan Doyle** worked it with Holmes (and the lesser-known but entertaining Professor Challenger), **Agatha Christie** with her stable of detectives.

As Hitchcock pointed out, the suspense of the traditional mystery is furnished through the intellectual puzzle. The reader vicariously filled the role of the sleuth, often in competition with the fictional sleuth to solve the crime first. The "whodunit" ruled. Along the way, the sleuth might have to figure out the "howdunit" before he got to whodunit.

In 1931, **Anthony Berkeley Cox**, writing under the pen name Francis Isles, turned the traditional mystery on its head by giving away the murderer right away. In *Malice Aforethought*, the husband, a conniving little shit, poisons his wife at the start. No puzzle, no mystery. What? Where's the suspense in that? Cleverly, Cox tossed aside the riddles of the whodunit, and plugged in a higher level of suspense provided by "we *know* whodunit, but will the bastard get away with it?" An emotional level had attached itself to the husband.

Over the years, readers came to demand a higher literary quality, peopled by more rounded characters. Increasingly, the goal became not so much "whodunit" as "whydunit." Psychology, human feeling, motives became as or more important than just the puzzle. It's unlikely you'll find a pure traditional whodunit in contemporary fiction.

This evolution naturally led to the "Suspense" genre. Puzzles become decidedly less important (though still exist), but the defining trait in the genre becomes the threat of danger.

Interestingly, the traditional whodunit made a big comeback in the form of the "cozy" mystery. Readers understandably can overdose on violence and danger, and long for something that will challenge them without grossing them out. The cozy is like an old friend, a polite one without the sex, violence, and profanity, and a great number, probably even the majority, are told in a humorous voice.

The modern thriller depends heavily upon action, fast pacing, and high stakes, often with a time element and multiple characters (although not always). The threat of danger abounds, often punctuated by violence. Thrillers are subdivided into a multitude of sub-genres… medical thriller, legal thriller, techno thriller, science thriller, military thriller, and a whole bunch more. Again, in their zeal for labels, the marketing folks have overdone it, and indeed will market almost anything that involves a crime as a thriller. One author joked that she expected to soon see a genre label called "knitting thriller."

Nonfiction Suspense

As mentioned earlier, *Apollo 13*, a nonfiction book and movie, keeps me on the edge of my seat. Clearly, in modern storytelling, a writer of nonfiction has at her disposal all the tools of suspense. The techniques we'll learn in the second part of this guidebook can be readily applied to nonfiction. Just because something is "true" (as nonfiction erroneously often claims), doesn't mean it can't be exciting.

Academics, fearing they won't be taken seriously by other academics, often still insist on writing in dry, lifeless style. This disappoints. Lifeless prose cannot breathe life into the subject matter. Storytelling *can*, and yields a better rendition of the truth than does a mere recitation of facts.

Among my favorite suspenseful nonfiction books are *The Hot Zone* by **Richard Preston** (1994), *In the Heart of the Sea: The Tragedy of the Whaleship Essex*, by **Nathaniel Philbrick** (2000), *Midnight in the Garden of Good and Evil*, by **John Berendt** (1994), and *The Monster of Florence*, by **Douglas Preston** and **Mario Spezi** (2008).

PART II: Building Suspense

Enough about the nature of suspense and its place in literature. Let's learn the tips, tricks, and techniques of building and sustaining suspense in our writing.

Research

Research is as essential to fiction as it is to nonfiction. Even pure fantasy, in which completely new worlds are constructed and peopled, will almost always require background knowledge—perhaps of metallurgy, or of cooking over a fire, or of masonry—and therefore research.

If the goal is to maintain suspense, research is vital to understanding and communicating. The spell one weaves in fiction is tenuous and easily broken. Once broken, it might be difficult to get it going again. An easy breaker of spells is getting the details wrong.

Some of your readers *will* know your subject matter better than you. They'll spot the mistakes. They might shrug and keep reading. They might not. They might go on the Internet and tell the world you have no idea what you're talking about. In any scenario, someone loses. At the least, their reading experience suffers, and that's not you want. Getting it wrong interrupts the momentum, and the spell of suspense is broken.

Don't just write that Agent Bob picked up a pistol if it's a revolver you describe. Know the difference. Do the research. The info is out there.

When it comes to research:

- The library is your friend. It's one of the great gifts of civilization. Use it. Librarians want to help, and if they don't have the books you need, they can probably borrow it or obtain it.

- The recognized expert is your friend. When I needed background on dental forensics for my novel *Brigands Key*, I sat down with my dentist, whose hobby was dental forensics and history, and picked his brain. I asked specific questions about techniques and materials used in the 1940s, about how they differ from current practices, and about how they might be identified. It was the least painful visit to the dentist I've ever had. I've also corresponded via email with medical examiners, a maritime law historian, and a Coast Guard archivist. They are flattered to be asked for help.

- Experience is your friend. If you're writing a Western, learn to ride a horse. If you're writing a survival tale, go camp in the wilderness for a week.

- Travel is your friend. If you're writing about a people or a place, visit them and it. It's fun and— wait for it— tax deductible.

- The Internet is your friend that can't be trusted. Seriously. The Internet is a good starting point for ideas, as with Wikipedia. But don't trust it. Any tinfoil-hat whack job can post anything on the Internet. Always find alternate, reliable sources. On the Internet, the reliable sources seem to be the college-related sites, the ones with the *.edu* suffix.

- Your friends are your friends that can't be trusted. Love your friends. Have a beer or six with them. But, unless they are experts in a particular field, do not trust their data, subject knowledge, opinions, earnest expressions, or anything else. Watching *CSI Miami* does not make your drinking buddy a forensics expert. Take it for what it's worth, and then find the recognized experts' writing on the topic. If you hurt your friends' feelings, buy them another beer or six. They'll get over it.

Start Strong

In any genre, get off to a good start. The first pages set the tone, style, setting, and voice for a story. It may be even more important in a suspense story than in most other forms, because you not only establish tone, style, setting and voice, you must also introduce something intriguing or suspenseful, if not flat out dangerous.

Great opening sentences yield great starts. Consider the following first lines of novels:

> *We were about to give up and call it a night when someone dropped the girl off the bridge.*
>
> —*Darker Than Amber*
> John D. MacDonald (1966)

MacDonald goes on in the next couple of sentences to explain that his boat bum sleuth, Travis McGee is fishing underneath a bridge in the Florida Keys with his buddy, Meyer. But the story has been launched with a girl wired to concrete being thrown from the bridge above. No time to consider consequences or mull over existential philosophy. McGee dives in.

> *They threw me off the haytruck about noon.*
>
> —*The Postman Always Rings Twice*
> James M. Cain (1934)

Think about that opener for a moment. Unlike the MacDonald opener, it doesn't specifically launch an action of the story. It instead paints, in a mere eight words, a portrait of the protagonist and his current station in life, and raises questions (and suspicions) about him in the mind of the reader. Imagine the difference Cain had written *I got off the truck at noon.* The starting point remains the same, but without the built-in questions and suspense. That's some damned good writing.

One-sentence opening lines are great, like a quick left jab at the opening bell, but of course an effective start can build over a longer span.

> *No one would have believed in the last years of the nineteenth century that this world was being watched keenly and closely by intelligences greater than man's and yet as mortal as his own; that as men busied themselves about their various concerns they were scrutinized and studied, perhaps almost as narrowly as a man with a microscope might scrutinize the transient creatures that swarm and multiply in a drop of water. With infinite complacency men went to and fro over this globe about their little affairs, serene in their assurance of their empire over matter...*
>
> *Yet across the gulf of space, minds that are to ours as ours are to those of the beasts that perish, intellects vast and cool and unsympathetic, regarded this earth with envious eyes, and slowly and surely drew their plans against us.*
>
> *The War of the Worlds*
> —H.G. Wells (1898)

So a few rules are in order. In the first chapter, if not the first scene, page, paragraph, or sentence…

- Get to the action.
- Set the tone.
- Establish the setting.
- Introduce the main protagonist.
- Give her a challenge.

As an alternative to introducing the main protagonist, set up a prologue or scene that presents something grim happening to a lesser character. In **Dan Brown's** *The DaVinci Code* (2003), the first scene involves a chase and murder in the Louvre. The protagonist, Robert Langdon, is not introduced until the next scene.

Prologues inspire different reactions in readers, agents, and editors. Some agents tell their clients to stay away from prologues, that they're passé, that everyone hates them. Which is rubbish. A prologue is just one a particular aspect of a story. If it's important to the story, and well executed, by all means include it. If it's nice, well executed, but not particularly important, it's probably a good idea to ditch it.

Hollywood is big on prologues, as you've noticed. And by and large, they are handled well. Can you imagine if *Raiders of the Lost Ark* (1981) ditched the prologue? The movie would suffer, and although the sequence wasn't particularly necessary to the rest of the film, it cleverly introduced and developed with visual shorthand both Indy and the villain that would resurface later.

I recently read a thriller (that shall go unnamed) by a bestselling author. The novel opened with a gripping prologue that took place several decades before the rest of the story, and that was by far the best part of the novel. Afterwards, the story suffered from over-the-topness. We'll talk about that later.

Create Characters We Care About

Every agent, editor, and publisher will tell you there's nothing new under the sun. They get flooded with dozens or hundreds of manuscripts every day, and chances are that they've seen every story idea, no matter how outlandish, pitched to them dozens of times by different writers. What makes them jump on one is not usually the idea or concept, it's the story, and story is all about character.

A school for wizards? I'll bet they'd all seen that one before **J.K. Rowling** hit the colossal big-time. What made hers stick is that you really pull for Harry, Hermione, and Ron. You care. Without that essential ingredient, suspense doesn't have much of a chance. Why invest emotionally in someone you could not care less about?

Create Flawed Protagonists

Part of creating characters we care about is creating characters who aren't perfect. We're all flawed individuals (present company excepted, of course).

Fans of Superman, I'm sorry, but the truth hurts. Superman is super boring. Batman is not.

When Superman was created, he basically had no flaws, no weaknesses. After a little while, his creators realized what a god-awful character he was, and came up with kryptonite as a way to give him a weakness. It wasn't much of an improvement. You still have a guy that flies with no apparent mechanism to do so. He doesn't even have wings. Or a rocket belt. It's stupid.

Anyway.

Batman is a regular millionaire guy with fancy gadgets. If you shot him, he'd die. Nothing special about him, really, and he's also a dark, brooding, disturbed cat. That's interesting. His creators actually put in a little thought before drawing him.

So bear in mind, protagonists aren't perfect. We don't want perfect. Look at time-tested protagonists:

- Sherlock Holmes, as written by Doyle, was an obsessed, anti-social, arrogant, drug abuser with hoarder tendencies. In spite of this, he was fastidious, unless stimulated by the intellectual challenge of a new case. Then he'd let himself go. Originally, he was much more clean-cut, but Doyle realized he needed to be roughened up a bit. Later, the movies sanitized him in the **Basil Rathbone** portrayals, and that was the widespread image of him, much to the series' detriment. The more recent **Robert Downey, Jr.** portrayal of Holmes hits much closer to true.

- Sam Spade, the hardboiled sleuth of **Dashiell Hammett's**, was a cynical, callous womanizer. Miraculously, John Huston managed to keep his rough edges intact in the movie version.

- Hercule Poirot, **Agatha Christie's** little Belgian, was fastidious and vain. I must admit that I've never been a big Christie fan, and would have liked to have seen Poirot's personal habits amplified even more.

- Special Agent Aloysius Pendergast, the FBI super-sleuth concocted by **Douglas Preston** and **Lincoln Child**, is an odd duck. Brilliant, but uncomfortable with human closeness and contact, harboring inner demons even he is reluctant to confront. He cares deeply for those around him, but has difficulty expressing

> it. Sometimes you want to throttle him, sometimes you want to hug him.

Give Antagonists Complexities

No character should be a cardboard cutout, and that includes villains. Even the worst among us probably have a few redeeming qualities. And the very nature of evil should compel the writer. What causes evil? How does it feel? How do good and bad occupy the same brain?

Aloysius Pendergast's nemesis and evil little brother, Diogenes, is a black-hearted fiend, no two ways about that. But the more you learn, you realize that he was warped by childhood trauma caused by his older brother. Evil, yes, but not because he wanted to be.

Faber (aka *die Nadel*), the German spy in **Ken Follett's** *Eye of the Needle* (1978) is a remorseless killer, but only in service to his country. He seems to actually feel for the innocents he kills or maims. You hate him, but a part of you respects him.

This is not to say that horrible persons should be made into heroes or anti-heroes. I'm always a little uncomfortable with the idea of a hitman being cast as the lovable hero in some stories. We do need role models, even fictional ones, and casting a criminal in a good light may not exactly fulfill the writer's responsibilities to humanity. And yes, we have responsibilities.

We're trying to build a society worthy of existence here, people.

Vary Sentence and Paragraph Length

Good writing comes with varied lengths of sentences and paragraphs. If too many sentences have roughly the same length, a monotony emerges. Most writers will "hear" the problem as they read their work and pounce upon and correct it for a more fluid sound. Moreover, varying and shortening certain paragraphs and lines helps to highlight action and build drama, calling attention to the things you want.

In my short story, "The Wreck of the *Edinburgh Kate,*" a small band of salvagers enter the deep recesses of a ship that has run aground off their little island, with only a crew of skeletons:

> *Amid the clutter, orderliness caught his eye. A stack of clothes, folded neatly, sat underneath the stairs, bound together with twine. Sanborn stooped to inspect the clothes; despite the neat, almost fussy folds, the clothes were grimy. Typical of a seaman's clothes, infrequently washed.*
>
> *He realized that none of the skeletons they'd found had even a tatter of clothing amid the bones. Each had been stripped.*
>
> *He led the group deeper into the hold, searching first the fore rooms, the sick bay*

and crew's mess, and working their way slowly aft.

Two more skeletons awaited in the midshipmen's berth, again with the cut marks of butchery.

At last, they reached the captain's cabin. Sanborn pushed open the door.

More disarray. Another skeleton lay in a dark wet corner.

The skeleton slowly turned to face him.

The skeleton is of course not a dead man at all, but the sole survivor on the ship, emaciated and starved near to death. I wanted to heighten the tension and drama and zero in on the moment of discovery, and varied the sentence structure as Sanborn and his party near this point. Seven paragraphs make up the passage. The length of each paragraph in this passage varies in this order:

- **Paragraph 1**: 44 words… This is the setup, a more leisurely pace. A good cop, Sanborn makes his observations.

- **Paragraph 2:** 22 words… Sanborn feels the ramifications of his observations.

- **Paragraph 3:** 25 words… He resumes his search.

- **Paragraph 4:** 15 words… More observations, more gruesome discoveries.
- **Paragraph 5:** 12 words… Closer…
- **Paragraph 6:** 10 words… Closer…
- **Paragraph 7:** 7 words… Key moment.

I didn't count words as I wrote this; I went by feel. The paragraphs and sentences grow shorter. The effect, psychologically, is that of a countdown. The reader feels something coming, something important, *before* they find the survivor. I hope that's the case, anyway.

Compress the Timeline

The structure of a story hinges quite a bit on its fictional time frame. A multi-generational **John Jakes** saga, for example, might take a century, and allows for a multitude of characters and storylines. Most novels take place over a span of days, weeks, or months.

Outline the plot and story you want to tell, and assign a clock or calendar to the benchmarks of the outline. Once it all makes chronological sense, consider shaving time off each part. Having a compressed timeline kind of forces the action and builds suspense inherently. Maybe you've plotted the story out on a calendar and figure it begins in Richmond, Virginia, runs about four weeks of fictional time, and concludes in Mexico City. Why not revisit the schedule and squeeze the story down into two weeks, or one? If all the plot points you deem necessary can be squeezed in, you've got built-in tension, easily achieved.

Start the Clock

Even more tension-inducing than compressing the timeline is the introduction of a deadline. Let events race against the clock. This is a common— some say vital— device in thrillers.

Suppose, in the timeline compression example above, you start again in Richmond in late April, but now you must be in Mexico City by Cinco de Mayo, or else all hell breaks loose. Now your readers and your protagonists are all in it together, watching the clock, knowing there's no time to screw around. Nothing makes things happen like the pressure of a deadline.

Deadlines don't have to be as overt as stating that **Quetzalcoatl** will rise from the earth at high noon on Cinco de Mayo, chug down a 1,000-gallon tanker full of *Dos Equis* (he doesn't always drink beer, but, you know…), and lay waste to the countryside. Deadlines can be stated, and very straightforward; or unstated… and more subtle.

Like the Quetzalcoatl example, a stated, straightforward deadline might say that Princess Patty must be rescued and whisked to the palace before Shoemaker Sam is hanged for her murder at noon on Saturday.

An example of an unstated deadline can be found in *Relic*, by **Douglas Preston & Lincoln Child**. Early in the novel, there are allusions to a coming gala event at the natural history museum, the event of the year, in which all the moneyed and powerful elite in New York will be present, despite the gruesome spate of "museum murders." The reader knows that this event looms as the end of the clock.

In **Ken Follett's** *Eye of the Needle*, the deadline is stated, but changes. German spy Die Nadel stumbles upon a top-secret ruse of the Allies and *must* get the information back to the Fatherland, posthaste. He must make his escape rendezvous. The British intelligence *must* catch him before he escapes England. As situations change in the story, the characters' own deadlines change.

Deadlines aren't limited to the overall structure of a novel, though that's where they're most recognized. The writer can work smaller deadlines into individual scenes or chapters, or into a short story, giving greater impetus to a particular part, and with little or no bearing on the larger structure. Thus, there may be different levels of deadlines to be met.

There might also be a deadline which affects characters within a scene, but of which they are unaware. Recall Hitchcock's explanation of the clock on the wall, ticking away, the audience fully aware of the looming explosion, even though the characters in the scene are not.

Bend Time and Space

Einstein proposed that time and space are not truly separate entities, and more importantly, that they are flexible. Writers understood this long before Einstein was a gleam in his papa's eye. Regardless of real world time, make unimportant passages take little or no time, and important passages take a lot.

For example, your protagonist drives to Orlando International, checks her bags, boards her flight, waits, flies to Atlanta, waits, eats chicken fingers, wonders what kind of chickens have fingers, waits some more, catches a connecting flight, and arrives at London's Heathrow Airport the next day. This takes eighteen hours. Guess what? Unless that long sequence of real-life drudgery somehow is integral to the story, as if, say, a mobster is watching her every move, and takes the seat right behind her, nobody cares. Most of us have endured the Atlanta airport and don't want to think about it. Write the entire scene in a line or two, or not at all.

Upon her arrival at Heathrow, a gunfight breaks out in baggage claim, and rages for two minutes. *This* is what we came for and stuck around for. Milk this section for five pages, eight pages, ten pages. Describe it in minute detail. The whistling of a bullet past her face, plucking at her collar, can take place in a microsecond, but can be described in an entire paragraph.

Vary the Pace

In music, softer, quieter passages heighten the drama and impact of the big numbers. In turn, the big, loud, fast numbers heighten the impact of the quieter passages. It's all about contrast and dynamics, and the same is true in storytelling. Readers need to catch their breaths. No action is boring, but nonstop action can also bore.

A flaw in a lot of action movies these days is the nonstop barrage of action and violence, and this has crept into some thrillers. Prose has a sort of built-in braking system, in that you can only read so fast, and reading speed varies amongst us. That's a good thing. As a rather slow reader, I think that contributes to my attraction to fast-paced storytelling. Even with built-in engine braking, action scenes too long and too frequent get a bit overwhelming. Suspense doesn't require fast-paced action, but action punctuating suspense can work wonders.

Avoid Going Over the Top

Another suspense killer can be going over the top, and asking readers to swallow too much. As a fan of the old TV series, *Mission Impossible*, I was excited to see the movie version finally come out in 1996. My excitement lasted about twenty minutes into the flick before the completely unbelievable action scenes lost me. Tears of boredom flowed for a while after that, and I finally stopped watching altogether. Now **Brian De Palma** is a great director and possesses a gift for suspense, so why did he throw that gift in the trash and go for slam-bang unbelievability? Is this what happens when directors get more budget than they should? In his defense, this was the project and script handed to him.

I read a bestselling thriller recently in which similar nonsense happened. By the midpoint, the action had simply gone beyond the pale of believability, and most of us (those with imaginations, anyway) are willing to suspend disbelief to quite a high level. I finished reading the book, but I doubt I'll give the author another try.

I say all this with trepidation, as I ask readers to suspend quite a bit of disbelief with my novels. It's fun to push the outside of the envelope; it's hard to know when you've ruptured it.

Stretch the Suspense

Building suspense by stretching it out is an obvious cure to going over the top in action sequences. Hitchcock understood this, as evidenced in the explanation on the difference between surprise and suspense he gave us earlier.

He demonstrates this brilliantly in *The Birds* (1960). In one scene, Melanie Daniels (played by **Tippi Hedren**) has already witnessed the dangerous and aggressive behavior that's suddenly afflicted the birds around Bodega Bay. She heads to the schoolhouse to talk to Annie (**Suzanne Pleshette**). She takes a seat on the bench to wait outside while teacher and kids rehearse some never-ending song. She lights a cigarette, and smokes nervously. Cut to the monkey bars in the playground behind her. A couple of crows land. The song goes on. A couple more birds land. The song by this time has become the most annoying song you've ever heard in your life, high, repetitive, and saccharine. More birds. The song just won't stop. You want to yell, "Look behind you! The birds!" The song goes on and on. You scream, "Will you little brats *please* shut your pie-holes?" Finally, she notices a single crow winging past her, she stands, watching it, fear in her eyes. She follows it, watches it land on the electric wires behind her. By now, there are hundreds of crows, sitting silently and watching her.

I believe Hitchcock intentionally sought out the most annoying song he could find, and made the viewing audience endure it as the crows gather. Not much actually happens, just a woman sitting on a bench, smoking, while birds gather and nasally children drive you nuts with their horrible song. Then tension piles higher every second.

Write Short Chapters

Let's face it. We modern readers have short attention spans. Television and movies have made us this way, and now the Internet has driven the stake into our once-patient hearts. By and large, we don't like long chapters in fiction. We skim ahead to see how close to a chapter end we are.

Many genre novels frequently have exceedingly short chapters. Less than ten pages. Sometimes six pages. Five pages. Three. I sometimes see chapters of not more than a paragraph or two.

Short chapters tend to keep readers flipping the pages. It's an easy and effective trick, particularly when you're using multiple viewpoint characters, but I caution against overdoing it. You pick up and purchase a novel, and glance to see that, hey, it's 406 pages long. You get into it and see that there are a hundred and fifteen chapters, each a few pages long, with half-pages of blank space at the beginning and end of each chapter. The book should have rightfully been maybe one-hundred eighty pages long. Feels like a sales gimmick. I would recommend not stringing together back-to-back chapters of only a couple of pages each.

End Chapters on Cliffhangers

In genre fiction, it pays to end each scene or chapter with a cliffhanger. Well… not necessarily a cliffhanger, but a hook of some sort. A new revelation, a new question, a twist, a pithy quote, a new conflict… *something* to make the reader say, "Okay, maybe just a few more pages tonight."

In my novel, *Brigands Key*, one chapter sends the protagonist, Carson Grant, venturing into the teeth of an approaching hurricane, and diving onto what he hopes will solve the mystery that has plunged the island into chaos:

> *Grant gripped the lamp and pointed downward. All he could see was blackness, a peculiar clear blackness, with flecks of white drifting and surging through.*
>
> *The primeval gut-fear of the unknown ran through him. Blackness, water with no bottom.*

> *Down he went, fighting the current, sweeping all directions with the beam of his lamp.*
>
> *The slope came into view. To his right, the craggy limestone plunged into the depths at forty-five degrees. Sea fans clung to it, waving in the currents, and sponges and urchins gave it an otherworldly beauty, brilliantly colored, starkly shadowed in the glow of the lamp.*
>
> *He followed it downward.*
>
> *Forty, fifty, sixty feet. Equalizing the pressure in his head. Seventy...*
>
> *And then he saw it.*
>
> *He stared in disbelief, forgetting to breathe.*

I originally wrote this scene to completion, so the reader immediately found out what Grant saw on the sea floor that caused him to momentarily forget all his dive training. In revisions, I saw that this was the perfect place to end what was becoming a long chapter. The reader's curiosity has been piqued and he's not stopping now. I hope.

Foreshadow

Foreshadowing is the art of hinting that things are coming. It may be done in action, thought, speech, prophecy, opinion, symbolism, metaphor, or other method. It's a valuable tool in fiction and has been for centuries, and all great writers use it.

Foreshadowing builds suspense by letting the reader know that something is looming.

For a story that might be far-fetched or asks the reader to suspend disbelief, foreshadowing is invaluable. If your story involves stuff way outside the realm of what we consider rational or real, you may find that you have to convince readers of lesser imaginative powers to hop on board. Most readers are willing to suspend disbelief, but it helps to ease them into that state of suspension. With foreshadowing, you can subtly introduce the concepts so that the reader is ready and accepting when they arrive.

If a story features action or tension that may take a while to develop, foreshadowing can add a level of suspense to get you there.

> *Winter came early and hard that year. It would be Admiral Velikovsky's last.*

After a line like that early in a story, you could spend an entire novel getting around to Velikovsky's end. The readers know it's coming, but if handled well, will sustain a level of suspense throughout. As Hitchcock demonstrated, the audience can be informed.

The opening of *The War of the Worlds* we examined earlier, in addition to being a killer opening, foreshadows like there's no tomorrow. It sets a stage of human hubris and arrogance and pretty much says the great disillusionment is coming, about to knock us off our flimsy perch. And by slipping in the reference to microscopic "creatures that swarm and multiply in a drop of water," it even foreshadows the ultimate vanquisher of the hostile aliens.

Write Dialog that Crackles

A literary novel I recently read, one touted by critics for its scintillating dialogue, held just the opposite for me. The heroine would think about something just said to her, think about her response, respond in a longwinded manner, and then ponder what she'd said. And pretty much everything she said was what you expected her to say. The person with whom she was speaking would then respond with an equally longwinded statement. The whole thing came off like persons lecturing each other.

I wanted to scream.

Dialogue can and should propel a story. I see no reason for an author to have her protagonist explain what she said. Just say it. It's what people do. But the thing is, even less than explaining to me what she said, leave even more unstated, and unexplained.

Those unsaid things in dialogue, the hidden messages, the unobvious answers, are what makes dialogue crackle with electricity.

It's doubly important in sustaining suspense.

The dialogue in the 1983 film *Gorky Park*, based on **Martin Cruz Smith's** 1981 novel, crackles throughout. Rarely do the characters say exactly what they mean. Unspoken threats, challenges, double-meanings, and accusations are hurled. I love it.

In one scene, Soviet inspector Arkady Renko (played by **William Hurt**) approaches rich American businessman Jack Osborne (**Lee Marvin**) in a bathhouse. Renko introduces himself in a chummy way and then all but accuses Osborne of being the one who brutally murdered and skinned young people in Gorky Park. Osborne, smirking, all but admits to it but hints that Renko is way out of his league and not smart enough to catch him. The exchange continues, neither saying what he really means, but the meanings are perfectly clear. Brilliant writing of dialogue, and the scene is electric.

Throw in a Little Sexual Tension

One of the most primal, gut-level issues of suspense might be summed up in a simple question: Will they or won't they? This has been the stuff of gossip and stories since time immemorial. We *want* to know if the characters will have romantic sparks, romantic drama, and ultimately, sex.

The urge to sex is elemental. Sometimes, of course, it just doesn't fit a story and is an obvious add-on, particularly in movies. Some movies based on novels have a tacked-on romance, where none existed in the novel. **H.G. Wells**' *The First Men in the Moon* comes to mind. There was no love interest in the book, not even a female principal character. The 1964 movie threw that in, to no improvement. Some studio exec deemed it necessary for the bottom line. He was wrong.

Well handled, sexual tension adds a lot, but must be woven into the overall fabric of the story. Watch *Gone With the Wind* (1939). The chemistry, absent from Scarlett's relationship with milquetoast first husband Charles, constantly smolders whenever Rhett saunters in. Will they or won't they? The question hangs in the air.

Note that I say "sexual tension," not "sex." Sex scenes, unless integral to the story, tend to slow or stop a story. Just my opinion. In the 1970s, it seemed that just about every popular novel had steamy, graphic sex scenes tacked on. I get that the sexual revolution was underway, so writers felt obligated to prove they were hip and crowd the plot with sex. These books got tedious in a hurry, and thankfully, popular fiction hasn't been dominated by this for a couple of decades now. Readers and writers got bored, grew, and moved on.

On the other hand, *Fifty Shades of Whatever* sells a lot more copies in a day than I sell in a year.

Throw in a Body

This is not an original thought on my part. Not at all. But it's certainly good advice, at least in the realm of the mystery, suspense, or thriller genres. Most novels have a discernible beginning, middle, and end. In suspense writing, it's safe to say that most novels feature a murder (or at least a dead body) in the beginning, to get things rolling.

The novel beginning can be a fairly lengthy chunk. It establishes principle characters, starts the plot, sets the tone, creates a setting or universe. This could be twenty-five percent of the novel. The end makes up maybe another twenty-five percent. The middle is the bulk of the story, and this is that fifty percent that can bog down.

If it *does* bog down, it may very well need a major plot development or revelation to keep the suspense alive. A dead body fits the bill. Keep one handy.

Throw in Little Complications

Life is a shitstorm of frustration. We're adults here, we can admit it. Things never go as smoothly as you think and as you plan. You buy a chair. You have to assemble it. You take it home and begin assembling. The instructions were translated by someone well-schooled in Mandarin, but not English. You muddle through anyway, only to find two pieces missing. You end up duct-taping the damned thing together. You sit on it three times and it collapses. *Grrr...*

Such is life.

The good news is, you can take these same little complications and place them in the way of your protagonist. It sounds like a minor, insignificant thing to do, but I can't stress it enough. There's almost no better way to raise momentary tension in a scene than to screw with your protagonist.

These really are the little things. A door knob gets stuck, a floorboard creaks, a computer crashes… just as your protagonist is struggling through a tense scene. Anything to make his situation more serious.

Follow Good with Bad

To elaborate on the little complications, a guiding principle should be to follow good with bad. And then follow bad with worse. If Protagonist Pete finally reaches the cockpit in time to save the doomed airplane after the pilot has died of a heart attack, consider sweetening the pot by having the right engine catch fire. Bad follows good. Then maybe the left engine flames out. Worse follows bad. This concept is related to the Little Complications, but these are clearly not little. A Little Complication would have been if the door got stuck when Pete tried to get inside.

Don't be nice to your characters. Be a jerk. You're their god; be an angry, vengeful god. Be heartless. It's fun. The Golden Rule doesn't work in storytelling.

Mae West provided the mantra for this. "When I'm good, I'm very good. But when I'm bad, I'm better."

Twist and Shout

Keep protagonists and readers off-balance throughout the story if you can. Once they start to think they're figuring things out, change it up for them. And when they solve one problem, have it lead to another (preferably worse) problem.

In *The Eagle Has Landed* (**Jack Higgins**, 1975), the German commandos think they've got things going well for their espionage mission in the English countryside… and then everything changes for both them and the locals when one of the commandos saves a child from drowning.

This act of compassion jeopardizes the mission, but allows the townsfolk to reevaluate their hatred of the enemy. Likewise, the Brit-hating Irish Republican Army operative, Liam Devlin, finds himself falling for a local girl, throwing all his carefully laid plans into disarray. This novel is also a great example of imbuing your antagonists with redeeming qualities and bringing them to life.

Throw in a Big Surprise

As your protagonists and readers inch ever closer to solving the mystery… make it something completely unexpected. Writers commonly create the surprise ending, but that can become a cliché' in a hurry if overused. Many readers even feel cheated or tricked by surprise endings.

My belief is that it's more important to suddenly shift gears earlier in the novel. Good places to pull this off are at the end of the novel's beginning, say 25% into the story. The readers have been introduced to everyone, can see the story set up, are comfortable with the ins-and-outs, and think they know which way the thing is going.

Shake them out of that comfort zone. If they've been led to believe your wife, the heiress, died in a 2014 plane crash in the first chapter, maybe she could reappear on screen in a 1922 silent movie that the hero happens to take in on impulse while tearfully walking the streets of Manhattan.

Another good place to go with the big surprise is at the end of the lengthy middle section. Things have continued apace, the story is clipping along quite nicely, thank you very much, but maybe you want to shift into fifth gear as you head into the final. Maybe the silent film actress is really a recurring six-dimensional holo-being from the future.

Reintroduce Their Worst Nightmares

Stephen King once wrote that a surefire way to make readers squirm would be to write about something bad happening to eyeballs. The eyeball is small and squishy and gross, and people cringe when eyeballs get hurt. King may be on to something. I nearly lost an eye once when I was a kid. I still remember the intense pain. Had to wear a friggin' eyepatch for quite a long time, and it was just a big white wad of bandage, nothing cool like a pirate's eye-patch.

There are dozens of phobias. There are phobias people have that make me laugh. I don't know if anyone has ever studied this, but I imagine that nearly everyone has an unreasoned fear of something. It makes sense that a handful of phobias are shared by a majority of us. "Us" meaning readers.

Reintroduce your hero (and your reader) to his or her worst nightmare. As already mentioned, almost everyone experiences fear to some degree. Some of us experience very specific fears, sometimes irrationally.

Phobias are inherent in most of us. Often the source of comedy, they can be serious, even paralyzing. Some, like agoraphobia— a fear of being out amongst the crowds in public spaces— strike most of us as abnormal, but make perfect sense to those afflicted with them. The person that suffers from agoraphobia might delight in the company of spiders. Go figure. There's no amount of rationalism and Zen calmness that could ever induce me to handle spiders and snakes. They're flippin' creepy.

If most of us have some phobia or other, it makes sense to capitalize on them in fiction. I doubt writing about agoraphobia is going to grip many readers, but it will certainly grip a very few, and if well done, offer some sort of vicarious suspense in the rest of us.

The more common phobias offer a rich vein of suspenseful ore. If a great number of us suffer common phobias, then it makes sense to play on those fears. Sure, it's the work of a jerk, but we need to take advantage of all our tools.

Among the more common phobias, we find deep-seated fears of the following:

- Heights (acrophobia).

- Snakes (ophidiophobia).
- Spiders (arachnophobia).
- Blood (hemophobia).
- Close Spaces (claustrophobia).
- The Dark (nyctophobia).
- Flying (aviophobia).
- Drowning (aquaphobia).
- Being Eaten (phagophobia).
- Clowns (coulrophobia)

And my personal favorite, Being Eaten by Clowns in the Dark. Stephen King's Pennywise the Clown manages that in *It*. I don't think that one's ever been assigned a name, so I'll invent it right now: *phago-coulro-nyctophobia*.

Many of us have phobias we don't even realize. One might not believe he has a fear of the dark until he's suddenly in absolute darkness in a manhole. Maybe it's a double whammy, with claustrophobia thrown in. The mind goes to work, concocting the worst that can happen.

And anyway, phobias are not necessarily unhealthy. Fear of snakes has a darned good evolutionary basis.

It's easy to work these things into a story, sneaking them in so the reader doesn't feel manipulated. Frightening scenes occur frequently in the dark, for good reason. The dark plays upon an inherent, primal fear, instilled in the species since the beginning. The dark is dangerous. Predators hunt in the dark. The dark *will* kill you. How can darkness not imbue a level of suspense into prose?

So go with it. If your protagonist fears heights, make him rescue his girlfriend from the top of a communications tower. In a lightning storm. If fear of drowning strikes terror into her heart, make her swim through a surging, flooded sewer. With rats.

Reintroducing a character to her worst nightmare doesn't necessarily mean a common phobia. It can involve a personal demon, a trauma from her past. If she hates her drunken, abusive mother, have the cartel kidnap her drunken, abusive mother, and force her to overcome her hate and attempt a rescue.

If he once killed a kid in an auto accident while dozing at the wheel, force him to stay awake three consecutive nights while driving a busload of schoolchildren over the ice-slicked roads of the Peruvian Andes, pursued by Shining Path guerillas.

Kill Passive Verbs

This is *Writing 101*. The syllabus says to keep passive verbs—*is, was, were*—to 10 or 15%, tops. They're too easy to be any good, and they murder storytelling. Figure out another way how to phrase what you want to say, with active verbs. Show it.

Although, as in anything, there are exceptions, and often the passive verb just *sounds* right.

> *They were the best of times, they were the worst of times.*

Dickens no doubt fretted over that opener for days, but in the end it sounded right. We're making art here, folks, and the writer's ear sometimes trumps *Writing 101*. Again, use the passive sparingly.

Avoid Negative Sentence Structure

Readers don't care what *didn't* happen. We care what *did* happen.

> *The rabbit did not run slowly.*

What a stupid way to say "the rabbit ran fast." Granted, that's an obvious example that no sane writer would use, but it illustrates the point of negative sentence structure. When prose is peppered with "not" (and its contraction cousins, "didn't," "wouldn't," "couldn't," and "won't,") it tends to apply the brakes. Brakes have never helped suspense or any other storytelling.

Some limited use of the negative doesn't hurt (see, I used it in this sentence), but keep it minimal. It seems to function a little better in dialogue, as it mimics accurately the way we converse, but probably should be reined in even in dialogue.

Always Create Tension

Remember now the great truth of fiction: conflict *is* story.

Strive for conflict in every scene, even when the characters are on the same side. We all want things to go smoothly and skate through without conflict, but that's a terrible recipe for storytelling. That's not to say that all characters have to be at odds with each other at all times. That might come across as contrived.

Conflict is not always in-your-face conflict. Conflict can be subtle and understated.

Conflict is not always between characters. Conflict can be between the protagonist and a squeaky hinge on a door (one of those little complications). Or with nature. Or with himself.

Internal conflict sometimes involves tough, even impossible choices. Make the cynical bar owner send the love of his life back to her husband. Rick overcomes his love and lust for Ilsa, knowing full well that she is his for the asking, but he knows the troubles of two little people don't amount to a hill of beans in this crazy world. There are far greater things at stake.

It worked in *Casablanca* (1942).

Make the private eye turn in the woman he's falling for. Sam Spade doesn't *want* to send Brigid O'Shaughnessy Up the River to the Big House, the Slammer, the Joint, the Hoosegow, the Pokey… but he does, because justice and his sense of duty to his murdered partner demanded it.

Worked in *The Maltese Falcon* (1929).

Make the young mother choose between her two little children which to save from the death camp. Talk about your impossible choices. Sophie faces the most impossible of all, and must choose to sacrifice one child in order to save one, and it destroys her.

Worked in *Sophie's Choice* (1979).

Make the POW blow up his beloved bridge so that the enemy can't use it.

Worked in *The Bridge on the River Kwai* (1952).

Apply the Techniques of Suspense

We now own a selection of tools for building suspense. Time to apply them to a straightforward passage.

In your story of intrigue and espionage set in Berlin in early 1937, your British protagonist, a housewife named Caroline, runs afoul of the local authorities. Her husband is jailed and interrogated by the Gestapo, through no fault of his own.

Caroline needs evidence to help free him, and resorts to a little B & E to get it. We take a first stab at the scene:

> *Caroline found the empty warehouse. She glanced about, opened the door, and entered. She didn't hear any sounds of movement inside. There in the corner was a file cabinet. She opened it, found a file labeled June, 1934. She rifled through the sheets, and located the list of names and dates she needed.*
>
> *She left the warehouse and hurried back to her car.*

Caroline's scene moves the plot forward, but without a lot of suspense. Everything goes too well for her; nothing but good news for her. It's a bit thin, too, more of an outline than anything else. So let's apply some tricks of the trade. Let's do the following:

- Start the clock.
- Compress the timeline.
- Stretch the suspense.
- Kill the passive verbs.
- Kill negative sentence structure.
- When "good" happens, follow with "bad." When "bad" happens, follow with "worse."

- Offer glimpses of hope.
- Shorten sentences and paragraphs to heighten drama.
- Reintroduce her to nightmares.
- Throw in little complications.
- End on a cliffhanger.

Caroline slipped inside the empty dark warehouse. She moved softly, measuring her steps. Outside, the rain fell, masking the sound of her movements. She glanced at her watch; in just seven minutes, the guard would make his rounds.

She found the file cabinet, tried it. It resisted, squeaking in protest. She pulled harder. The lock held. She spotted a pile of debris, selected a rusty piece of steel, jimmied it into the edge of the file drawer, and leaned hard into the steel. The cabinet sprang open with a loud snap. She stole another glimpse at her watch. Four minutes left. Still plenty of time. She rifled through files and found one labeled July, 1936. She withdrew the list of names and dates she needed and turned to go.

The rain stopped.

A soft sound, a crunch, barely audible. From outside. Footsteps. A yellow glow flickered through a crack in the door. Caroline caught her breath; the guard had begun his rounds early. He rattled the latch, eased open the door, shone his flashlight inside.

Caroline cast about, desperately searching for another exit. Blank walls lined the interior.

She looked up. Eight feet above the floor, a glint of light marked a broken window, slightly ajar. A way out! She ran to it, jumped, and caught hold of the sill and pulled herself up. A shard of glass fell from the sill and stabbed her forearm, and shattered on the floor. Caroline gasped, clawed the air, fell.

A low growl rumbled across the floor. She twisted toward it. A Doberman strained at its leash, broke free, and raced toward her.

Caroline scrambled to her feet, slipped in her own blood, and crashed again to the floor. Wrenching pain seized her knee. No chance of outrunning the Doberman.

She felt about, found a shard of glass, spun, and slashed at the beast as it slammed into her.

Okay then! We've wrung suspense out of a flat scene. Let's break it down to illustrate how the techniques have been applied.

Caroline slipped inside the empty dark warehouse. In the very first sentence, we've introduced a common phobia, simply by making it dark.

She glanced at her watch; in just seven minutes, the guard would make his rounds. We've started the clock, just for this one little scene. The reader now has a timeline implanted in her thoughts.

She found the file cabinet, tried it. It resisted, squeaking in protest. She pulled harder. The lock held. We give Caroline momentary success—finding the cabinet easily—but follow it with a little complication. The damned thing won't open, and even makes noises when she tries it. Bad follows good…

She stole another glimpse at her watch. Four minutes left. The time element hangs over her, and we're losing time.

She withdrew the list of names and dates she needed and turned to go. Ah! Sweet success! Hope is restored!

The rain stopped. Uh-oh. A complication. Caroline's movements are no longer masked by the sound of the rain.

A yellow glow flickered through a crack in the door... the guard had begun his rounds early. The clock just got short-circuited.

Caroline cast about, desperately searching for another exit. Blank walls lined the interior. Things just got worse.

She looked up. Eight feet above the floor, a glint of light marked a broken window, slightly ajar. A way out! Ah, a spark of hope!

She ran to it, jumped, and caught hold of the sill and pulled herself up. Yay! I think she's going to make it!

A shard of glass fell from the sill and stabbed her forearm, and shattered on the floor. Caroline gasped, clawed the air, fell. D'oh! Bad follows good. The writer is a jerk.

A low growl rumbled across the floor. She twisted toward it. A Doberman strained at its leash, broke free, and raced toward her. The Dobie is a variation on the phobia against being eaten. It's an animal with a bad attitude and sharp, fangy teeth.

Caroline scrambled to her feet... Yay!

... slipped in her own blood, and crashed again to the floor. D'oh! Why do bad things keep happening to nice people? We *like* Caroline.

Wrenching pain seized her knee. D'oh!

No chance of outrunning the Doberman. Translation: no chance of not being eaten, or at the very least not being ripped to shreds.

She felt about, found a shard of glass, spun, and slashed at the beast as it slammed into her. A tiny sliver of hope… and then we end the scene on a cliffhanger. Damn you, Mr. Writer-Man!

In the interest of brevity, I kept this revision short. If I were to rewrite this again, I'd draw out the quiet parts longer, stretching them out as Alfred Hitchcock suggests, prolonging the suspense. In particular, the point at which Caroline realizes the guard is poking around could and should be drawn out longer. Any good film director would know how to play with the details of light and shadow there, the beam of the guard's flashlight playing through the cracks, sliding across the floor like a living creature, sniffing her out. These are moments of drama to be exploited.

Closing Arguments...

Storytelling has its roots in suspense. It's likely that the first stories ever told were suspenseful, giving respite to the clan gathered about the warmth and safety of the home fires of prehistory. Despite the harshness and danger endured in their daily lives, our distant ancestors relished the entertainment value of real tales of the hunt or the battle, told by scarred and grizzled old hunters, their voices raising and lowering, peppered with embellishments and whole fictions to get the wide-eyed youngsters leaning in just a bit more.

Suspense is vital to fiction, regardless of genre, regardless of style, though it varies in degree from genre to genre, from story to story. For the literary-minded, don't be afraid of suspense. Read **Hemingway's** powerful short story "The Short Happy Life of Francis Macomber" (1936) if you doubt me. Suspense is a life force, it's malleable, and it can be stretched, tightened, whipped, and pounded. And then reused or recycled. It's sustainable!

As pointed out at the start, suspense is related to fear, and fear is not a bad thing. Fear can actually be pleasurable, yielding as it does rushes of blood and adrenaline, and sweet release from the unpleasant feelings once the agent of fear passes. This is why we ride roller coasters and dive with sharks. When we understand that we can't be hurt, such as when we read a book or watch a movie, the intensity of fear is much lower than that which we experience in actual life-threatening situations; the emotional payout may be lower, but the investment (your metaphorical ass, rather than your literal ass) is also much lower, so the entertainment value remains a bargain.

Suspense should be built into the structure and plot of a story. If not, there's perhaps little that can be ladled on in the way of details that will make the story great. Conversely, if the suspense is built into the overall structure, but the details of suspense are lacking, the story might not be all it can be. Good news is, those details can be easily added.

Mastering the techniques of suspense is not the end-all of good suspense writing, of course. The elements of good writing always apply, and always come first. Write well, write better, apply the techniques of suspense, and you'll have the makings of a page-turner.

And if you get tired, take a break and watch a little Hitchcock.

Then, rising with Aurora's light,
The Muse invoked, sit down to write.

—Jonathan Swift, 1733

I hope you've found this guidebook helpful and possibly even entertaining. It'll be much appreciated if you could post a review online at websites for readers and writers.

For a companion guidebook on the essential skills of point of view, take a look at ***Out of Sight, Out of Mind: A Writer's Guide to Mastering Viewpoint***, available online.

Thanks!

—*kp*

About the Author...

Ken Pelham lives and writes in Maitland, Florida. His thriller, ***Brigands Key***, won first place in the Florida Writers Association's Royal Palm Literary Awards and was published in hardcover in 2012 by Cengage/Five Star Mystery. The ebook edition hit the electronic shelves in 2013.

Brigands Key is "...a perfect storm of menace...breathtaking!"
--*The Florida Weekly*

Ken's follow-up novel, ***Place of Fear***, also a first place winner of the Royal Palm Literary Award, was published in 2013.

Also available for e-readers online:

Treacherous Bastards: Stories of Suspense, Deceit, and Skullduggery
A collection of three stories in the Hitchcock tradition, including one about the little island of Brigands Key.

A Double Shot of Fright: Two Tales of Terror
Two chilling short stories guaranteed to cause loss of sleep.

Tales of Old Brigands Key
Three short stories about the strange little island and its somewhat unsavory past.

Ken is a member of Florida Writers Association and International Thriller Writers. Visit him at **www.kenpelham.com** for updates on his work, and musings on suspense fiction.

www.ingramcontent.com/pod-product-compliance
Lightning Source LLC
Chambersburg PA
CBHW032140290326
41933CB00058B/605

* 9 7 8 0 9 8 9 5 9 5 0 4 9 *